The News Never Stops

John DiConsiglio

www.raintreepublishers.co.uk
Visit our website to find out
more information about
Raintree books.

To order:
☎ Phone 0845 6044371
▤ Fax +44 (0) 1865 312263
✉ Email myorders@raintreepublishers.co.uk

Customers from outside the UK please telephone +44 1865 312262

Edited by Adam Miller, Andrew Farrow,
  and Adrian Vigliano
Designed by Steve Mead
Original illustrations © Capstone Global
  Library Ltd
Picture research by Elizabeth Alexander
Originated by Capstone Global Library Ltd
Printed in China by South China Printing
  Company Ltd

ISBN 978 1 406 21760 5 (hardback)
14 13 12 11 10
10 9 8 7 6 5 4 3 2 1

**British Library Cataloguing in
Publication Data**
DiConsiglio, John
The news never stops. – (Mastering media)
070.4'3-dc22
A full catalogue record for this book is available
from the British Library.

Acknowledgements
We would like to thank the following for permission
to reproduce photographs: Alamy pp. **12** (©
Chuck Mason), **30** (© Irene Abdou), **35** (©
Boitano Photography), **42** (© NetPics); Corbis
pp. **6** (© H. Armstrong Roberts/ClassicStock),
10 (© Bettmann), **16** (© Toby Melville/Reuters),
18 (© Corbis), **20 right** (© Bettmann), **26** (©
Corbis), **29** (© Mark Peterson), **36** (© Rick
Maiman/Sygma), **38** (© Andy Rain/epa), **39 top**
(© Rune Hellestad), **39 bottom** (© Peter Foley/
epa); Getty Images pp. **4** (Joe Raedle), **7** (Ralph
Crane/Time & Life Pictures), **8** (Boris Horvat/
AFP), **15** (Hulton Archive), **20 left** (Hulton Archive),
21 (David Hume Kennerly), **22** (John Moore), **24**
(Arthur Cofod/Pictures Inc./Time Life Pictures), **32**
(NASA/AFP), **34** (CBS Photo Archive), **44** (CAREL
PEDRE/AFP), **46** (SHADISHD173/AFP), **48** (Dan
Kitwood); Photolibrary pp. **19** (Norbert Michalke/
imagebroker.net), **40** (Carlos Cazalis/arabianEye);
© Yousef A. Raffah p. **47**.

Cover photograph of a US tank destroyed in
Baghdad, reproduced with permission of Getty
Images/Mirrorpix.

We would like to thank Devorah Heitner
for her invaluable help in the preparation
of this book.

Every effort has been made to contact copyright
holders of material reproduced in this book. Any
omissions will be rectified in subsequent printings
if notice is given to the publisher.

Disclaimer
All the Internet addresses (URLs) given in this

Contents

Some words are printed in bold, **like this**. You can find out what they
mean by looking in the glossary.

Breaking news

Dateline 1990

You are a reporter with a **scoop** – a news story you will be the first to report. You are in Baghdad on the eve of the first Gulf War (1990–91). US missiles bombard the Iraqi capital. On a rooftop overlooking the city, your cameraman trains a lens on you. Millions of people around the world switch on their televisions. They watch you report on the war as bombs explode behind you.

Dateline 2005

You are a reporter with a scoop. Three bombs have exploded on the London Underground. An hour later, a double-decker bus is bombed. You are the first to interview police on the scene. You quickly write up your notes. Your report will appear in tomorrow's edition of the *Guardian* and almost immediately on the newspaper's website.

Dateline 2010

You are a reporter with a scoop. You have heard that a famous athlete has failed a drug test. You click on your computer and quickly post the rumour on your Internet **blog**. In less than a second, it is available around the world for people to read on computers and on "smartphones" like iPhones and BlackBerries. It sets off a flurry of posts on social networking sites like Facebook and Twitter.

Welcome to the world of 24-hour news.

As these examples show, the way news is reported has changed remarkably in recent history. The changes over the last few centuries have been even greater. From the printed page to television cameras to the Internet, technology has transformed news-gathering, as well as the news itself.

The telegraph

Until the 1840s, most news travelled no faster than a horse or a ship. The **telegraph**, an electric wire that carried messages the same way phone lines do, sped things up greatly. Even then, it often took days or weeks for news to reach readers.

Newspapers and magazines were the leading news sources of the time. When the passenger ship the *Titanic* sank in 1912, only one newspaper carried accounts of the disaster – and it was more than a day after it happened.

Reporters rushed to make newspaper deadlines in the early 1900s, but news still travelled slowly.

The revolution of radio and television

By the 1920s, radio revolutionized the news **industry**. People turned the dial on the radios in their living rooms and heard staticky descriptions of world events as they happened. In the 1950s, television brought the sounds and pictures of the news into homes.

Television revolutionized the news industry. Now the world could see news events, like this press conference from US President John F. Kennedy.

"Radio and television gave you an immediacy [sense of being there] that you never had before," says Ohio University **journalism** professor Patrick Washburn. "Suddenly you could be anywhere in the country and if you could see a television, the news came to life for you."

The rise of the Internet

In the late 1990s and 2000s, the Internet plugged the news into a whole new world. With websites, blogs, and social networking services like Twitter, news is now available all the time. Today, anyone with Internet access can be wired into almost unlimited sources of news.

What is news?

But what is news, exactly? Charles A. Dana, a **journalist** from the 1800s, defined it as "anything that interests a large part of the community and has never been brought to its attention before". In other words, news is new. It is what people are talking about. Author Evelyn Waugh said, "News is what the chap who doesn't care much about anything wants to read".

Journalism is the reporting of news. Traditional journalism – whether it is a newspaper article or a television report – is based on the "five Ws": who, what, where, when, and why. Those are the five most important questions in a news story. A journalist should answer those questions within the first paragraph of an article or, on television, within the first few seconds of a report.

Public scenes of reporters fighting for a statement only represent a small part of the journalism process.

Avoiding bias

In theory, journalists are taught to never take sides on an issue. They are trained to tell the story exactly as it happened. However, not all stories are reported equally or from the same perspective. Reporters can have a **bias**, meaning they support one point of view, based on the type of news they report and the kind of **media**, or news outlet, they work for (see box below).

How does bias work?

To understand how bias works, let's look at a case of a famous athlete who is accused of failing a drug test for steroids. An army of reporters might pounce on the story. Each one could see it from a different angle:

- A news reporter might seek out the facts: when was the athlete caught? What was the drug he used? Is the test reliable?
- A sports reporter might focus on the impact on the athlete's team: will he be suspended? For how long? How will his team replace him?
- A financial reporter might look at the economic outcome of the story: will the athlete be fined? Will he lose his shoe company contract? What will happen to the team's ticket sales?
- An entertainment reporter could look at the more personal side of the story: what does the athlete's film star wife think? Will they still attend exclusive parties? Does the public still like them?

In each case, the reporters are doing their jobs, and they are probably trying their best to tell the truth. However, they are delivering the news to different audiences – news seekers, sports fans, money managers, and star-watchers. They tailor their reports to suit those audiences.

A journalist's code of ethics

Journalists should follow a certain code of ethics, or rules. These rules include:

- Seek the truth and report it fully.
- Look for different perspectives. In other words, report on all sides of an issue.
- Do not report on any story if you have a personal connection to it. For example, if it involves your friends or family or a group that you belong to.
- Do not be influenced by anything but the truth. Do not let powerful people change your mind, and do not accept gifts from anyone.

News or gossip?

Throughout the history of journalism, reporters have not always been able to keep bias out of their stories.

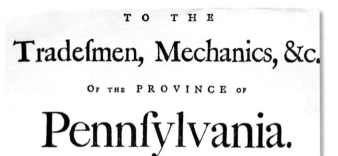

This 1773 colonial newspaper printed criticism of British taxes instead of unbiased news.

In the 1700s, European newspapers were generally fair. But some people used printed documents to argue for specific causes. The poet John Milton distributed pamphlets opposing religious discrimination. Jonathan Swift, the author of *Gulliver's Travels*, printed attacks on Britain's abuse of the poor.

Journalism barely existed in the United States before the American Revolution (1775–83). This was the time when the United States fought against Britain and won its independence. The earliest printed news was mostly gossip and opinions. Many newspapers and pamphlets were designed to spread political ideas.

The next century saw a more traditional news world, one in which reporters – or newspapers, radio stations, and television networks – were expected to stick to the facts. However, as we will see later in the book, bias still often creeps into all kinds of reporting.

Magazines

The United Kingdom took the lead in the magazine world. London's weekly *Penny Magazine* started in 1832. It ran longer, more in-depth articles than newspapers. British magazines also began using illustrations to accompany articles. The *Illustrated London News* may have invented war correspondents when it sent reporters to cover the 1899 Boer War in what is now South Africa.

Libel

What happens when a journalist lies? That is called **libel**. It can cause a lot of damage to a journalist's career and reputation.

What can people do if they think a journalist has "libelled" them? Let's go back to the athlete who tests positive for steroids (see page 9). What if the reporter was wrong, and the athlete never failed the drug test? The athlete could sue the reporter for libel and take her to court. If the athlete won the case, he could collect a lot of money from the reporter and her employer, whether it is a newspaper, television station, or website.

Libel can be very hard to prove. The athlete would have to show that the reporter lied on purpose, and that she did so to harm the athlete. If the athlete could not prove those points, he would lose his case.

Newspapers and magazines change the media world

Newspapers are still produced on giant printing presses.

US President Thomas Jefferson once said that if he had a choice between government without newspapers or newspapers without government, he would choose the newspapers.

More than 200 years later, newspapers are still, in many ways, the backbone of **journalism**.

Before radio, television, and eventually the Internet, newspapers were the fastest way to spread word of major events. For example, when an earthquake rocked San Francisco, USA in 1906, readers around the world read the details about it in their newspapers, although not until nearly a week later. At the time, that was considered fast-moving news!

Throughout the rest of the century, people across the world depended on their daily paper to catch up on **global** events. Today, many people still buy newspapers as they travel to work.

Watchdogs and crusaders

There are many different kinds of newspaper and magazine **journalists**, as we will see in this chapter. Many of them often see themselves as watchdogs. They keep an eye on governments and powerful people to make sure they are not abusing their roles. From South America to South Africa, reporters have **crusaded** for public freedoms.

Crusading can be dangerous for all types of journalists. A non-profit group called Reporters Without Borders supports the rights of the **press** all over the globe. The organization reports that in 2009 alone, 76 journalists were killed and 573 imprisoned for their work. Most often, journalists face these dangers in poor countries or those without a strong tradition of freedom of the press.

The "Penny Press"

In the 1800s, the popularity of European and US newspapers rose dramatically. The Industrial Revolution, a period when machines and factories began to be widely used, was flourishing. This meant papers could be printed quickly and cheaply. A new postal system meant that newspapers were also easier to deliver. The invention of the **telegraph** allowed reporters to rapidly relay news to their paper's headquarters.

In 1833 Benjamin Day opened the *New York Sun*. It was the first "**Penny Press**" – a cheap daily newspaper. The "Pennies" drew readers with **sensational** reports on murders, sex, and **scandals**. The number of US newspapers skyrocketed from 3,000 in 1860 to 7,000 in 1880. Big cities like New York and Chicago had as many as 10 newspapers that reached 15 million people.

Yellow journalism

As newspapers grew, reporters fiercely tracked stories to feed the public's growing appetite for news. Some stories were spectacular, such as reports on the 1906 earthquake in San Francisco, USA or the 1912 sinking of the *Titanic*. Others were sensational, focusing on famous people's love affairs.

In New York City, USA, two rival **publishers** used their newspapers to change public opinion – and make themselves rich. At the turn of the century, William Randolph Hearst's *New York Journal* helped create US support for the Spanish–American War (1898). "War is good for **circulation** (the number of readers)," he said.

Across town, Joseph Pulitzer's *New York World* crusaded for the poor. Pulitzer attracted readers with wild headlines. For example, a story on a heat wave was entitled "How Babies Are Baked". Both publishers practised "**yellow journalism**", a style of writing that stresses eye-catching headlines and sensational details over hard facts.

Lord Beaverbrook

In the United Kingdom during the same period, William Maxwell Aitken (also known as Lord Beaverbrook) was an early star of "Fleet Street". The UK press got this nickname from the name of the street where it had its offices. In the early 1900s, Beaverbrook transformed dull newspapers into witty, colourful journals with eye-catching photo layouts.

William Maxwell Aitken (Lord Beaverbrook) was Britain's first media baron. In the early 1900s, he transformed dull newspapers into colourful journals.

Muckraking

In the early 1900s, many writers used their newspapers and magazines to expose government **corruption** and highlight unfair treatment of workers. They attacked big business and child labour abuses. US President Theodore Roosevelt called them "**muckrakers**". He said they never raised their head from the "muck" of the floor while searching tirelessly for wrongdoing to expose.

After World War I (1914–18), Beaverbrook's *Daily Express* was the most widely read newspaper in the world. Beaverbrook could make or break famous people by the way he instructed reporters in his newspapers to report a story.

Tabloid times

In the United States in 1952 Italian publisher Generoso Pope bought a horse-racing newspaper called the *National Enquirer*. He instantly shifted its focus from horses to horrors. He ran sleazy stories about gruesome murders and grisly deeds, with headlines such as "I cut out her heart and stomped on it!" and "I ate my baby!" The *Enquirer's* circulation quickly jumped to a million copies a week.

The **tabloid** era had begun. Tabloid newspapers were named for the large size of their pages. Taking yellow journalism one step further, they combined breaking news stories with celebrity gossip. Then and today, tabloids frequently report on the sex scandals of the rich and famous.

Tabloids like the *Sun* have high circulation by combining news with gossip and scandals.

What a scoop!

Reporters working for tabloids regularly get a **scoop** before more traditional journalists, and they expose public corruption and private problems. For example, in 2007, tabloids reported rumours that US presidential candidate John Edwards had an affair and fathered a child outside his marriage. The story, which turned out to be true, was not picked up by other **media** until two years later. In 2008, tabloids reported that pop star Michael Jackson was gravely ill only a matter of months before his death in 2009.

Is it news?

Are tabloids, with their focus on the sleazy and sensational, really news?

Many "mainstream" journalists would say no. They note that tabloids report on issues that may be popular with the public, but that are not really newsworthy. They also argue that, unless someone is breaking the law, the private lives of celebrities should remain private.

Tabloids have famously followed, even harassed, celebrities in search of scoops. Princess Diana was often surrounded by packs of tabloid reporters and photographers nicknamed "paparazzi". When she was killed in a Paris car accident while being chased by photo-seeking paparazzi, Britain's three leading tabloids admitted they were partially to blame. Tabloid coverage had, as the **editor** of the *Sun* put it, "created a frenzy and appetite around Diana" that helped contribute to her death.

Tabloid editors say they are just giving the public what it wants by aggressively pursuing stories that other journalists ignore. This is perhaps proven by the fact that tabloids are widely successful. The *Sun* has the highest circulation of any English-language daily newspaper in the world.

In the last 100 years, newsrooms have changed from cramped offices with click-clacking typewriter keys …

Inside the newsroom

Take a peek inside a busy newsroom. It is where news gathering begins. Reporters scurry from desk to desk. Editors bark out orders. The click-clack of typing fills the air.

Is this a scene from 2010 or 1910?

Newsrooms have certainly changed a lot in the last 100 years. Today's reporters write on computer keyboards – not typewriter keys. Televisions and Internet connections are on every desk. Almost all newspapers have their own websites. While most staff members are still men, more than 30 per cent of today's reporters are women.

But some things are still the same. At most newspapers, reporters sit at desks, collecting news and writing articles. Their stories are passed on to editors who review and even rewrite them. The editors also work with photographers, designers, and illustrators. These people work on the images that accompany a story and create the overall appearance of the newspaper.

Editorials

Flick through a newspaper. There are different sections for different topics: front-page news, fashion, business, sport, and more. Writers for all of these sections are expected to follow the journalism tradition of not being **biased**.

That is not true for the whole newspaper. Most newspapers set aside columns called "editorials". These articles are not supposed to be about listing facts. They express the views of the editors or owners. They state the newspaper's official opinion on important issues, such as who they think should win an upcoming election.

Climbing the pyramid

Imagine a newspaper article as an upside-down pyramid. At the top are the most important facts of the story: the five Ws, or who, what, where, when, and why. The details at the bottom, the pyramid's point, are less critical. That is the way that newspaper reporters are taught to write. It is a style called the inverted pyramid.

Why do they write like this? One theory is that busy readers do not have time to finish a whole story. All of the meaty news must be in the beginning. Others say that editors came up with the idea so they could easily cut articles that are too long. They would just have to chop off the fluff at the pyramid's point. Some say the style came from the telegraph. Before phones, reporters used the electrical wires to transmit stories to their editors. Telegraphs were unreliable and the most vital facts had to be relayed first, before the signal was lost.

... to modern newsrooms, equipped with computers, televisions, and state-of-the-art technology.

19

HEADLINERS:
THE NAMES THAT MADE NEWSPAPER HISTORY

Here are a few of the biggest names in newspaper history.

UPTON SINCLAIR

In 1906 US author Upton Sinclair wrote *The Jungle*, which told of horrific conditions in Chicago's meatpacking **industry**. Sinclair found that companies sold diseased food to the public.His book led to the first food safety and consumer protection laws.

C.P. SCOTT

C.P. Scott was the editor of the *Guardian* newspaper for 57 years from 1872. At that time, the paper was based in Manchester. Scott bought the paper when the previous owner died. The *Guardian* became well known internationally during Scott's time as editor. In a famous article he swore to continue the paper's independent tradition and said, "Comment is free, but facts are sacred".

KATHARINE GLASIER

Katharine Glasier was among the founders of the Independent Labour Party in 1893. She wrote columns in various publications including the party's newspaper, the *Labour Leader*. She edited the *Labour Leader* from 1917 until 1921. During this time circulation reached its peak of 51,000 copies. Glasier campaigned for the ILP across the UK and later set up the Women's Labour League.

ETHEL PAYNE

When Ethel Payne was a dedicated reporter

for the *Chicago Defender*, a leading African-American newspaper, she was given the nickname "First Lady of the Black Press". Payne fiercely supported civil rights for black people. She was a tough questioner and often angered US presidents like Dwight Eisenhower. When the Civil Rights Act of 1964 was passed, President Lyndon Johnson invited Payne to attend the law's signing.

PERCY HOSKINS

The lead crime reporter for the UK newspaper the *Daily Express*, Percy Hoskins covered the 1956 trial of John Bodkin Adams, a suspected serial killer who was thought to have murdered as many as 400 people. Hoskins believed Adams was innocent. But no one else did, including Hoskins' publisher, Lord Beaverbrook himself (see page 15).

Bob Woodward (left) and Carl Bernstein (right).

Beaverbrook considered firing Hoskins, until Adams was found not guilty of the crimes.

BOB WOODWARD AND CARL BERNSTEIN

Perhaps the most famous journalists ever are Bob Woodward and Carl Bernstein, determined reporters who worked for the *Washington Post* in the 1970s. Woodward and Bernstein uncovered corruption and crimes in US President Richard Nixon's administration and wrote about it in the *Post*. The scandal that resulted, known as the Watergate scandal, led to the unthinkable: Nixon became the only US president to ever resign from office.

Are newspapers dying?

Newspapers were once the fastest way to learn about world events.

Today, they seem as slow as the horse and cart. There is little news on the front page that has not already been covered by television news or websites.

From the dawn of radio in the 1920s to the beginnings of television in the 1950s to the explosion of the Internet in the 1990s, experts have asked: has technology left newspapers behind?

The final issue of a US newspaper, *Rocky Mountain News*. The newspaper closed in 2009 after 150 years in the business.

Changing times

Many newspapers are losing money, readers, and staff. Europeans are buying fewer newspapers. Circulation fell in 13 European nations in 2009, with the biggest drops in Ireland and the United Kingdom. More than 50 US newspapers went bankrupt from 2008 to 2009. Young people today are more likely to get their news from television or the Internet than they are from newspapers.

Some experts worry that a public without newspapers will be badly informed. They wonder what will happen if newspapers are not around to keep an eye on governments. Internet news and **blogs**, critics say, are filled with gossip rather than real reporting. (For more on this topic, see pages 43 to 47.)

New strategies

Still, newspapers are not giving up just yet. Newspaper sales are up in developing nations and new markets. China has recently seen a 4 per cent boost in its newspaper growth. India's newspaper circulation went up almost 9 per cent from 2004 to 2009.

Almost all newspapers have websites, most of which attract more readers than their print versions. More than 75 million people visit newspaper websites. Web audiences for newspapers around the world have grown by 350 per cent in the period from about 2004 to 2009.

While the Internet has brought them new readers, newspapers have not yet worked out how to make money online. The Internet versions of newspapers are usually available for free. Worldwide, newspapers make just 2 per cent of their money from the Internet. However, in 2010 *The Times* website began to charge people to view its content. It remains to be seen how successful the experiment will be.

"I have no doubt that there's still an appetite for the convenience of newspapers," says Helen Boaden, head of news for the BBC. "People are still going to want information, but newspapers are going to have to find new and innovative ways of getting to them".

23

Over the airwaves

When the *Hindenburg* burst into flames in 1937, people around the world heard the news immediately on the radio.

In 1937 a giant German airship called the *Hindenburg* was completing a flight across the Atlantic Ocean. As it attempted to land near New Jersey, USA, it suddenly exploded. The *Hindenburg* burst into flames, killing 35 passengers.

The news of the disaster spread immediately – but not by newspapers. Millions heard the *Hindenburg* crash as it happened. They heard it on the dominant **media** of the era: radio.

The rise of radio

By the 1920s, radio had matched newspapers as the most important source of news. In 1922 the BBC was the first company to **broadcast** experimental radio programmes. Radio listeners had to purchase a licence that helped to fund the BBC. By the end of the 1920s, three million licences had been bought.

At first, most radio **broadcasts** involved music and sports. The public tuned in to hear jazz singers like Al Jolson or listen to immensely popular 15-minute comedy programmes.

In the 1930s and 1940s, radio emerged as a source of instant world news. The BBC led the rise of news radio, following its **motto** to "inform, educate, and entertain". Instead of waiting for a morning newspaper, listeners now only had to turn on their radio.

Soon politicians and world leaders took advantage of the new medium. In the United Kingdom, King George V started the tradition of delivering a "Christmas message" to the country over the radio. His son George VI used a yearly radio speech to boost people's spirits during World War II (1939–1945).

In the United States, President Franklin D. Roosevelt used regular radio addresses, known as "fireside chats", to talk directly to the public. It helped him lead the country during the Great Depression (1929–c.1939) and World War II.

Radio goes to war

The scene is London, 1940. The sky is filled with bomb flashes and billows of smoke. Warning sirens cut through the night. Nazi Germany is bombing the city. This bombing raid is called the Blitz, and it will last for 57 nights in a row. More than 43,000 people will be killed. Millions of homes will be destroyed.

And you are there – sort of. From a rooftop high above the city, CBS News radio reporter Edward R. Murrow is describing the Blitz in gripping detail. Listeners around the world are glued to their radios.

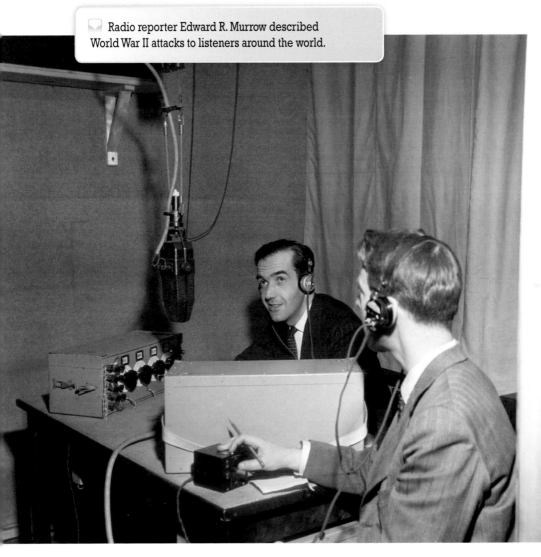

Radio reporter Edward R. Murrow described World War II attacks to listeners around the world.

Bringing the war home

Radio news reached its heights during World War II. Unlike newspapers, radio provided immediate coverage of world events. Murrow led the way. He reported on German leader Adolf Hitler's rage across Europe, and listeners followed his every step on their radios.

The propaganda wars

Radio was used for more than broadcasting news. Governments employed radio programmes as **propaganda**, meaning the broadcasts were meant to influence public opinion.

During World War II, both sides beamed propaganda over the radio. (The two sides of the war were the Axis powers, made up of Germany, Japan, and Italy, versus the Allies, made up of Great Britain, the United States, France, the Soviet Union, and others.) On the Axis side, Germany and Japan used the airwaves to spread messages against the Allies. Japanese radio beamed messages from a broadcaster named "Tokyo Rose". "Rose" was really 12 separate female broadcasters who tried to disrupt Allied spirits by predicting their gruesome deaths. Germany used the voice of a woman nicknamed "Axis Sally" to taunt homesick Allied soldiers by saying their families had deserted them. She mocked the important D-Day invasion by telling Allied forces, "The D of D-Day stands for 'doom'... 'disaster'... 'death'... 'defeat.'"

At the same time, the BBC broadcast messages of support to Allied troops throughout Europe. Announcers even sent code words to give instructions to Allied soldiers.

The new airwaves

Radio had become the king of news media but its reign did not last long. In the 1950s, television signalled the death of radio as the world's number-one news source. Suddenly the public would not settle for hearing events. It wanted to see them, too. (See pages 32 to 41 for more on television.)

Radio survived by specializing. Many stations changed from news stations to "Top 40" music channels and sports channels. In the 1960s and 1970s, BBC stations refused to play popular rock and roll music. As a result, hundreds of "pirate" radio stations beamed rock to UK radios. When the government tried to curtail their broadcasts, the "pirates" set up portable transmitters on boats.

Speech radio in the UK

The news did maintain a presence on the radio. Today, the BBC still provides radio broadcasts to 182 million people around the world across 33 language services. In the last three months of 2009 figures show that nearly 90 per cent of the UK population listened to the radio at some point.

While news is obviously available on a number of different media, speech radio is clearly a popular option. For example, Radio 4 (current news topics, debates, and interviews as well as drama) gets nearly 10 million listeners, 5 Live (focuses on news and sport) gets over 6 million and TalkSPORT gets 2.5 million listeners.

Fair no longer?

In the USA for many years, radio broadcasters of any news story or **controversial** issue had to be careful to fairly give both sides. If a commentator supported something, then someone who opposed the idea also had to have equal time on air. In 1987, the 1949 law that required this, known as the "Fairness Doctrine", was **repealed** after complaints that it violated US free speech rights.

On US radio stations today, **partisan** voices (who support a particular point of view) appear on many radio stations, giving their opinions on everything from politics to education to religion. Some of the most outspoken of these broadcasters are known as "shock

jocks", short for "shocking disc-jockeys". Most "shock jocks"
not only freely give their own opinions on air, but use a phone-in
format where others can join in the arguments! The most famous
US shock jocks are Rush Limbaugh and Howard Stern. In Australia,
shock jock Kyle Sandilands is the most controversial.

US radio presenter Rush Limbaugh uses his programme
to influence listeners with his right-wing political beliefs.

Radio Africa

Today's most thriving radio market is not in the United States or Europe. It is in Africa. Countries throughout the African continent are discovering that radio can be an important source of news, education, and even propaganda.

In many developing African nations, television is an expensive luxury. Newspaper delivery systems are often poor, and they reach only a small percentage of people, many of whom cannot read. On the other hand, experts say radios can be found throughout African villages and cities.

A group of young people in Burkina Faso display their radio.

Propaganda airwaves

The BBC's African stations beam news reports around the world. Local channels play a mix of music, news, and phone-in programmes.

African governments have also used radio stations as propaganda tools, not unlike European radio during World War II. In Liberia, dictator Charles Taylor gave radio broadcasts to keep his "iron fist" rule over the country in the 1980s. In Rwanda in 1994, government announcers encouraged people to kill members of other ethnic groups. They helped spark the violence that led to the murder of over 500,000 Rwandans.

Uniting nations

Today, some African nations are using the airwaves to help unite their people. A loosening of government restrictions has allowed Somalia to develop a small network of private and community radio stations. These stations are important communication tools in a country where many people cannot read and there are few newspapers.

In Sierra Leone, radio pioneers are using the airwaves to heal the wounds of the nation's decades-long civil war. Radio led the way in rebuilding the country's infrastructure in 2000. Sierra Leone had only three stations. That quickly grew into more than 20 stations. Today, 85 per cent of the population relies on radio for news.

Radio played a huge role in Sierra Leone's 2002 elections, the country's first free elections in decades. Radio commentators gave information about polling locations and acted as watchdogs for violence and voting problems.

Television takes over

Astronaut Neil Armstrong took "one giant leap for mankind" when he walked on the Moon. Back on Earth, half a billion people watched him on TV.

It is July 1969. The impossible is happening. A spaceship has landed on the Moon. A US astronaut called Neil Armstrong walks along the dusty surface. "One small step for man," Armstrong says. "One giant leap for mankind".

Half a billion people are witnesses, from more than 322,000 kilometres (200,000 miles) away. Back on Earth, an awed public huddles around their television sets to watch Armstrong's lunar landing. The age of television is in full swing.

Sights and sounds

The BBC began broadcasting in 1936 but very few homes had televisions at that time. Technical problems and high costs kept them from being widespread until the 1950s. It was the coronation of Queen Elizabeth II in 1953 that encouraged people to purchase televisions for the first time. Even then, many people just crowded into a neighbour's house to watch.

Newspapers had first informed readers of important events. Radio had then made news immediate. Listeners heard about events as they happened. Television took news to an unimaginably higher level. Now the sights and sounds of history – from the moonwalk to the assassination of President John F. Kennedy to the wedding of Prince Charles and Lady Diana Spencer – were experienced in living rooms.

Television changed the way people viewed everything from politics to sports. It also changed **journalism**. In 1989, Sky News became the first all-news channel in the UK. Suddenly, news really was available at any hour of any day.

The emergence of television news

The first daily television news bulletin was broadcast in 1954 on the BBC. ITV's flagship news programme, News at Ten, did not appear until 1967.

In the United States in 1962 a man named Walter Cronkite became the presenter of the CBS *Evening News*. He established himself as a fatherly figure. Cronkite became the most trusted person in the United States and known around the world.

Children's news

In 1972 John Craven's Newsround was shown on television for the first time. It allowed children to become more involved in the news because the programme was specifically directed at them. It was presented by John Craven and became famous for breaking news stories such as the Challenger Space Shuttle disaster in 1986.

In the 1960s and 1970s, TV news anchorman Walter Cronkite was known as the most trusted person in America.

Essential news

Television became central to major news developments. Political leaders became masters of using television coverage to announce major policies. Television also made people aware of the harsh realities of war. During the Vietnam War, viewers were shocked to see images of dead soldiers shipped home in body bags. These images stirred popular demands to end the war.

The rise of 24-hour news

During the 1960s and 1970s, television news stuck to a formula. Sometimes a special report might be run to cover a natural disaster or an election. Otherwise, news programmes used their regular evening timeslots and then "signed off", meaning they ended for the night and only updated the news again the next day.

In the United States, that changed on 1 June 1980, when US **media mogul** Ted Turner introduced the world's first 24-hour news channel. It was called the Cable News Network (CNN).

Rolling news in the UK

Sky News was the first 24-hour news channel in the UK. It began in 1989. The BBC's rolling news channel followed in 1997. In 2000 Independent Television News (ITN) set up its own 24-hour news channel as competition to Sky and the BBC. It later became the ITV News Channel, but closed in 2005 to make way for a channel dedicated to children's programmes.

A 24-hour channel that presents news from a European persective, euronews, is also available in the UK on satellite and cable television. It allows viewers to change the language that programmes are broadcast in, which means that it relies on a voiceover rather than presenters.

CNN was the most important television news innovation of its day. By 1985 CNN was in 30 million homes in the United States.

Rupert Murdoch and the news

In 1996 an Australian media mogul named Rupert Murdoch launched the Fox News Channel in the USA to compete with US channel CNN. The Fox News Network was Murdoch first step into television news in the USA.

After nearly 60 years of expansion, Murdoch's empire is still growing.

Murdoch's News Corporation company began with newspapers and magazines in Australia and New Zealand. He later bought major newspapers in the UK and the USA. In 1989 he started the first of his satellite television services, Sky Television, in the UK, followed by others elsewhere. He also owns cable TV channels, music companies, and Internet services.

Right or wrong?

Is it a good idea for one person to have control over so much of the news media in the world? Is it likely that the news will be biased because it is in one person's hands? To some people there is nothing wrong with news channels, like Murdochs' Fox News Channel, reflecting the owner's views, in Murdoch's case in favour of conservative causes and politicians. Others see a danger in opinions that are presented as news, which may confuse viewers.

Think like a critic!

Keep these key hints in mind when watching television news:

Beware buzzwords

See how one channel reports a news story versus another channel. Do they use different buzzwords? Buzzwords are words used to make certain ideas seem either negative or positive. You can often tell which side reporters favour by listening for a buzzword. For example, when discussing abortion, do they say *pro-life* (a buzzword for people who oppose abortion) or *pro-choice* (a buzzword for people who support abortion rights)?

Keep it in perspective

Whose point of view does the story represent? In 2009, a police officer in Boston, USA, had a confrontation with a black professor from Harvard University. Some news reports emphasised the officer's responsibility to keep the peace. Others noted that police abuse of minorities is all too common. An unbiased reporter must show both sides.

Cover me?

Whose opinion is being covered, or discussed, and how? Think about whether a reporter presents only one side of an issue. Did she interview people with different points of view? Did she give them equal time? Or was the coverage dominated by just one opinion? Remember: there are two sides to every story – and usually more!

Fair or foul? Spotting news bias

So, how do you know when a news report is fair, and when it is biased? Your best weapon is knowledge. If you keep up with current events, you can spot whether **journalists** are reporting them fairly.

This is the BBC

Today, in the United Kingdom, the BBC is the world's largest broadcasting news organization. It has a greater **global** reach than any other news service. The BBC has a news-gathering force of 2,000 journalists, and 70 bureaus based around the world.

The BBC is the world's largest broadcasting news organization, reaching 240 countries.

The BBC first broadcast television news in the 1930s. The service was suspended in 1939 because of the outbreak of World War II. Then in 1953, 27 million people watched live news reports of Queen Elizabeth II's coronation (crowning).

BBC critics take aim

By law, the BBC is required to be free from political and commercial (money-making) influence. BBC executives boast that they answer only to viewers and listeners. The network's well-known standards for journalism have earned it a reputation as one of the world's fairest news services.

Even so, the network's independence has been **controversial**. Governments have accused the BBC of being sympathetic to the nation's enemies. During the Cold War, when democratic nations like the United Kingdom opposed communist countries like the Soviet Union (now Russia), some felt the BBC favoured the Russians.

During the Gulf War against Iraq, anti-BBC politicians labelled it the "Baghdad Broadcasting Corporation".

Still, a recent poll ranked the BBC as the world's "best and most trusted provider of news".

Headliners: broadcasting legends

Here are a few of the biggest names in broadcasting history:

Pauline Frederick Robbins

Pauline Frederick Robbins opened the door for women to be taken seriously as journalists. Known as the "voice of the United Nations", she covered foreign affairs for US channel ABC for 7 years, NBC for 21 years, and National Public Radio (NPR) for 16 years, starting in the 1940s.

Kate Adie

Kate Adie made her name reporting for the BBC on the 1980 siege of the Iranian Embassy. At that time, she was one of the few women who reported from dangerous situations such as war zones. She became the BBC's chief news correspondent in 1989. She has won many awards for her reporting on major stories such as Tiananmen Square massacre.

David Frost

Known as "the Cronkite of Britain", David Frost is recognised as a great interviewer. He **scooped** all US media in 1977 when he became the first to interview US President Richard Nixon after he resigned.

Christiane Amanpour

The UK-born reporter Christiane Amanpour is the chief international correspondent for CNN. Television viewers have become accustomed to seeing Amanpour report from major crises in global hotspots such as Iraq and Afghanistan. Amanpour helped disprove the myth that women cannot report from war zones.

Al Jazeera: the voice of the Middle East

Television stations in the United Kingdom and the United States have earned their share of controversy. But no network has caused more controversy than the Middle Eastern station Al Jazeera.

Al Jazeera's name means "island" in Arabic. To some people, Al Jazeera is the most hated station in the world. To others, it is the most trusted.

The Al Jazeera TV network is trusted by many Arab viewers as a more unbiased news source than western media.

The Middle East does not have a tradition of journalistic freedom. Experts say that state-run television in many Arab nations is heavily censored and biased towards governments. At the same time, many in the region distrust western media. They think that UK and US stations are biased in favour of Israel and broadcast anti-Arab propaganda.

In 1996 Al Jazeera debuted from a studio in Qatar. It quickly gained a trustworthy reputation in the Arab world. Al Jazeera

broadcast the news that state-run television often banned. It also allowed opposing views that seemed to be missing from UK and US **broadcasts**.

Al Jazeera has rapidly expanded into a huge television and Internet network. It gained worldwide attention following the terrorist attacks on 11 September 2001 when it was the first station to broadcast live from Afghanistan, where terrorists connected to the attacks were believed to have been trained. Stations like the BBC and CNN often use Al Jazeera footage on their own programmes.

A strained relationship

The station continues to cause controversy in the West. It has angered US leaders by broadcasting videos from Osama bin Laden, the mastermind of the 2001 attacks. Both the *Guardian* newspaper in the United Kingdom and Fox News Channel in the United States have accused Al Jazeera of showing videos of masked terrorists beheading western hostages. However, that charge has never been proven, and the *Guardian* had to apologise.

In 2003 Al Jazeera's office in Baghdad was hit by a US missile, killing one of its reporters. This further strained its relationship with the West.

The news net: how the Internet is changing journalism

News has moved online. For better or worse, the Internet has become a powerful medium and changed the nature of journalism.

Early reporters like **muckraker** Upton Sinclair reached hundreds of people with newspaper and magazine articles. Radio pioneer Edward R. Murrow and television giant Walter Cronkite brought sounds and images into living rooms.

Even so, none of them could have predicted what a British computer scientist called Tim Berners-Lee started in 1991: the Internet, a **global** information space accessible to anybody with a connected computer. Berners-Lee simply wanted to make it easier for researchers to share their work. He had no idea that he was about to start a new phase in **media** history.

With the Internet, almost anyone can now find the news they want when they want it. With wireless technology, people in search of news do not even need a computer. Today, most news is also available on "smartphones" like iPhones and BlackBerries.

Problems and controversies

However, the new media model is not perfect. Many people around the world do not have Internet access. Only 7 per cent of Africa and just 19 per cent of Asia offer widespread Internet access.

Internet **journalism** has been **controversial**, too. To some, it has ushered in a new age of participatory journalism. This means that, thanks to the Internet, ordinary people are not just reading the news. They can also post comments on it, and even report it themselves on **blogs**. Many people see this involvement of ordinary people as a good thing.

However, some people warn that bloggers are not a substitute for well-trained **journalists**. As we will see, posting news on the Internet does not make it true.

43

Blogs

What are blogs? Short for "weblogs", blogs are online journals where people can write almost anything they want. Anyone with a computer, some simple software, and Internet access can start one.

In 2003, three-quarters of Internet users had never read a "blog". At the time, about 1 million blogs existed. Today, blogs are transforming journalism and politics. People who log on to the Internet can choose from about 100 million blogs worldwide. That number is growing all the time.

Bloggers: The new reporters?

Many blogs are no more than personal diaries. Other bloggers have produced journalism and social commentary. Writing from all different political viewpoints, people use blogs to break news stories and fire off political memos.

When Haiti was devastated by an earthquake in January 2010, citizen journalists took mobile phone photos like this one to provide some of the first images of the tragedy.

Blogs can influence other media coverage by checking facts and adding details to reports from major media sources. For example, in 2004, bloggers found mistakes in a CBS story charging US President George W. Bush with avoiding military service in the Vietnam War. It eventually led to the resignation of veteran journalist Dan Rather. Also, like **tabloids**, blogs often cover stories that other reporters ignore.

"Bloggers who practise journalism are journalists," says blogger Ana Marie Cox. "It's as simple as that". Proving the increasingly important role of blogs, bloggers like Matt Drudge and Arianna Huffington were among *Time* magazine's most influential people in 2006.

Citizen journalism

What is "**citizen journalism**"? It is exactly what it sounds like: ordinary people without professional journalism training using technology tools – from mobile phones to Internet blogs – to report and write their own news, or to fact-check and comment on other media reports. Citizen journalists might blog about an accident they saw on the street. Or they might investigate a news article and post the mistakes they found. Others may snap a video of a police arrest and upload it on to YouTube.

The terrorist attacks of 11 September 2001 were a turning point in citizen journalism. Many ordinary citizens became on-the-spot reporters of the attacks. They took pictures with their mobile phones and wrote personal accounts on websites and early blogs. In many cases, these ordinary people provided more complete news coverage than some professional journalists.

Standards and rights

Yet critics say blogs cannot always be trusted.

Just as with other types of news media, there are different kinds of news blogs with different kinds of standards. Some are written by reporters from newspapers or television channels. Some are written by self-proclaimed reporters and citizen journalists (see box on page 45). Too often, many argue, these non-professional journalists do not have training and are not careful enough about checking facts. Also, some bloggers may use their web space to advance their own **partisan** causes.

Blog supporters believe that mainstream reporters should not have the exclusive right to present a subject. They say ordinary people know as much, if not more, than reporters alone and should contribute to coverage.

People who support blogs also point out that blogs can be important tools in advancing human rights (see box on the right).

Blogs are only becoming more popular with time. Over 77 per cent of web users around the world say they read blogs. Top blogs attract more than 3 million visitors a month.

Many bloggers in Iran helped to organize massive street protests following disputed elections in 2009.

Blogging for freedom

Blogs are not just for diaries and advancing political views. They can also be tools for global human rights activists.

Bloggers have become the Internet voice of **dissent** in countries that do not allow basic freedoms. Human rights activists say blogs are important **forums** to challenge injustices by ruthless governments around the world.

Bloggers in danger

Many nations try to prevent bloggers from reaching large audiences. Bloggers have been imprisoned for posting anti-government messages in countries such as Egypt, China, Libya, and Iran. In fact, the group Reporters Without Borders estimates that 151 bloggers were arrested around the world in 2009 for posting comments critical of their governments.

Blogging has become a popular forum for dissent in Iran. There are 46,000 Iranian bloggers, including a large number of women. The Iranian government has responded by arresting bloggers, including journalists from some of the few newspapers not run by the state. Some of the bloggers are reportedly being held in solitary confinement and tortured.

In 2007 in Saudi Arabia, a popular young blogger was arrested for insisting on democratic reforms. Fouad al-Farhan used his blog to campaign for the release of imprisoned Saudi liberals.

Fouad al-Farhan, the popular Saudi Arabian blogger.

Where to now? The future of news

A Twitter user sends a tweet from Westminster Abbey in London.

From the printing press to the Internet, the news **media** has seen incredible changes in the past few centuries. **Journalists** have adapted to change, moving from the page to the radio and television dials to the Internet.

So, what's next? Certainly the newspaper world is in trouble. Newspapers are losing **circulation**, advertising, and subscribers. Some have even had to shut down. Many have tried to gain a new identity online.

Internet sites and cable channels have stepped in, along with websites and **blogs**, to fill the space left by newspapers.

Many experts think the future of news will look much like the present, but more so. Blogs have popularized the idea of "**citizen journalism**", of ordinary people reporting their own stories on blogs or Internet sites. Hand-held devices like "smartphones" will let people read and report the news from virtually anywhere.

Experts say this is hard for journalists to swallow. To some, citizen journalism is a dangerous next step from blogging. They imagine a media culture reporting unchecked rumours and gossip.

Others see potential in a news media that works with the public. Instead of news being reported by institutions like newspapers and television stations, experts see news models with everyday people participating in the media. In that wide-open model, citizens and reporters work together to ensure that the news is accurate and available to everyone.

One thing is certain: a new media model is coming. The ways we gather our news and the people who report it are bound to change yet again. However, one thing will not change. The news will keep coming. Whether we read it in a newspaper, listen to it on a radio, or watch it on a television screen or computer, the news never stops.

Timeline

1450 German inventor Johannes Gutenberg develops the printing press. For the first time, large numbers of books and other documents can be printed and distributed.

1665 The first British newspaper, the *Oxford Gazette*, is published.

1702 Elizabeth Mallet publishes the first daily newspaper in Britain, the *Daily Courant*.

1922 The BBC is formed.

1932 King George V delivers his "Christmas message" over the radio for the first time.

1937 The German airship *Hindenburg* explodes, killing 35 passengers. The disaster is heard live across the world over the radio.

1939 BBC television **broadcasts** are suspended during World War II. They resume in 1946.

1950 Children's Newsreel is shown on the BBC. It includes a lighter version of the news of the day.

1953 The BBC broadcasts the coronation of Queen Elizabeth II. People crowd into the homes of the few who own televisions to watch the spectacle. In total, nearly 20 million people watch the coronation, outnumbering radio listeners for the first time.

1954 Over 3 million homes now have television sets, but there is still only one channel until the emergence of ITV in 1955.

1963 President Kennedy is shot in Dallas, USA. Television coverage of the assassination and the funeral grip the nation and the world for days.

1969 US astronaut Neil Armstrong takes humankind's first steps on the Moon. The event is seen live by half a billion television viewers worldwide.

1970 The teletext system is developed in the United Kingdom. The news-retrieval system lets users call up news, sports, and weather updates on their televisions.

1972 The first news programme aimed specifically at children, called *John Craven's Newsround*, is shown on the BBC. With its name shortened to *Newsround*, it is still broadcast today.

1980 US **media mogul** Ted Turner creates CNN and broadcasts news 24 hours a day.

1989 Sky News becomes the first 24-hour news channel in the UK.

1991 British computer scientist Tim Berners-Lee puts the first website online.

1994 The *Telegraph* is the first national newspaper to go online.

1996 The Arab news network Al Jazeera debuts from a studio in Qatar.

2001 The 11 September terrorist attacks usher in the age of **citizen journalism**, as ordinary citizens snap mobile phone pictures and create **blog** coverage of the attacks.

2003 One million blogs are on the Internet.

2010 Experts estimate that as many as 100 million blogs exist.

Glossary

bias supporting one point of view, usually in an unfair way. Reporters try to avoid bias so that their stories are fair.

blog online journal

broadcast to transmit over the airwaves, like radio or television; also refers to a radio or television programme

circulation number of readers a newspaper has, based on the amount of copies sold

citizen journalism when members of the public play an active role in collecting, reporting, analysing, and spreading news and information

controversial causing a dispute or a strong disagreement

corruption lack of integrity or honesty

crusade to strongly advocate in favour of something

dissent protesting to show disapproval, usually of an action or law

editor person who determines the final content of a text, like a newspaper story

forum public meeting or a place to discuss ideas

global involving people all over the world

industry commercial enterprise; a business

journalism the collecting, writing, editing and presenting of news, whether in newspapers, radios, TV, the Internet, or other forums

journalist person who writes stories or broadcasts news

libel false and damaging statement printed in a publication. It is intended to damage a person's reputation.

medium (plural: media) means of communication, like radio and television, newspapers, and magazines

mogul extremely powerful business person; also might be called a baron or tycoon

motto a saying that expresses a principle

muckraker crusading journalist who exposed corruption in the early 1900s

partisan supporting one point of view

Penny Press nickname for the cheap daily newspapers that were wildly popular in the United States in the 1830s. Costing just a penny, the publications drew readers with sensational stories, but also allowed ordinary people access to news coverage.

press a term for the news media

propaganda broadcast or printed material meant to influence public opinion

publisher person or group who owns and prints a newspaper

repeal to undo a law that has previously been made

scandal public controversy

scoop exclusive news item that is first reported by just one news organization

sensational intending to arouse great interest or controversy

tabloid type of newspaper known for combining news stories with gossip, often focusing on celebrities' personal lives. The term comes from the size of the publications' paper.

telegraph electric wire that carries messages in the same way as phone lines. In the early 1800s, it allowed news to quickly travel over long distances.

yellow journalism style of writing that stresses eye-catching headlines and sensational details over hard facts

Find out more

Books

21st Century Science: Telecoms, Simon Maddison (Franklin Watts, 2007)

Global Industries Uncovered: The Media and Communications Industry, Rosie Wilson (Wayland, 2009)

Information Literacy Skills (series), Donald C. Adcock (Heinemann Library, 2008)

In the News: Freedom or Security?, Judith Anderson (Franklin Watts, 2006)

Media Power (series) (Franklin Watts, 2009)

Muckrakers: How Ida Tarbell, Upton Sinclair, and Lincoln Steffens Helped Expose Scandal, Inspire Reform, and Invent Investigative Journalism, Ann Bausum (National Geographic, 2007)

Websites

www.thinkuknow.co.uk/11_16/
Have a look at this website to learn about staying safe online and what new sites are good to visit.

www.rsf.org
Reporters Without Borders is a non-profit organization that supports the rights of the press around the world. It tracks reporters who have been imprisoned, injured, or killed while covering stories.

http://news.bbc.co.uk
This is the BBC's news website.

www.cnn.com
This is CNN's news website.

**www.bl.uk/reshelp/findhelprestype/news/concisehistbritnews/
britnewspaper.html**
This website has a timeline covering the history of British
newspapers.

www.tvhistory.btinternet.co.uk/html/landmark.html
This website has a timeline of UK television history.

**www.channel4.com/learning/breakingthenews/schools/
thestoryofnewsday/default.html**
This website tells the story of a day in 2005 when pupils got
together with the Channel 4 news team to create a news
programme. It includes a breakdown of what happens during the
day before a news programme is broadcast in the evening.

www.kidsmart.org.uk
Learn more about Internet safety on this website.

Topics to research
To learn more about the news, research the following topics:
- how a news programme is made
- how a news report is fact-checked
- citizen journalism
- censorship versus freedom of speech.

Index